Wildie Thayer

First Poems

Wildie Thayer

First Poems

ISBN/EAN: 9783744710916

Printed in Europe, USA, Canada, Australia, Japan

Cover: Foto ©Thomas Meinert / pixelio.de

More available books at **www.hansebooks.com**

FIRST POEMS

WILDIE THAYER

BOSTON
THE MORNING STAR PUBLISHING HOUSE
1895

As the message came directly
  From sweet Nature's heart to mine,
May it by some subtle process
  Gain access to heart of thine.

INDEX.

viii INDEX.

A Shell.

Pink-tinted shell,
Thy history tell,
O tell it all to me;
I bend my ear,
A sound I hear,
An echo of the sea.

Like memory's gleams,
Like mystic dreams,
A throb of Ocean's heart;
Thy secret well
Thou guardest, shell,
I know not what thou art.

To Nature dear
I bend my ear,
To hear her secret sweet;
But, like the shell,
She will not tell,
I hear her heart's loud beat.

To Nature given
A sound of heaven;
It throbs within her breast;
O bend thine ear,
And thou shalt hear
An echo of your guest.

The breath of God
Is in the sod,
His life is in the air;
I feel, I feel!
He does reveal
That he is everywhere!

Nature.

Do you ask me to tell you of Nature
　　When flowers are under your feet ?
If you'll look you can trace her quite clearly
　　In petals of flowers so sweet.

Do you ask me to tell you of Nature
　　When in stillness and darkness of night ?
Just see ! She is written above you
　　In stars shining coldly and bright.

Do you ask me to tell you of Nature
　　When her manner seems lonely and cold ?
List to the wind in its moaning,
　　'Twill all Nature's sorrow unfold.

Do you ask me to tell you of Nature
　　When her beauty seems almost divine?
List to the birds, they sing of her ;
　　Their language is sweeter than mine.

O listen for Nature ; she's calling
　　From tiniest dainty flower-bells.
No one can tell you of Nature,
　　For Nature her own story tells.

Haunted.

Children's hearts are filled with fancies,
  Filled with visions, phantoms fair,
Magic pictures, drawn by fairies,
  Hung in castles made of air.
Through their hearts roam ghosts impatient,
  Thoughts of future, dreams of fame.
Children's hearts are light and merry,
  But are haunted all the same.

Hearts of youth are strangely haunted;
  Ghosts from fairy-land appear:
And they whisper gently, " There are
  Brighter spirits lurking near."
Thoughts of life, of love, and passion
  Haunt their hearts, ah, sadly true!
Hearts of youth are fiery, loving,
  But are haunted through and through.

Hearts of manhood, filled with power,
  Passion, life, are haunted yet—
Haunted by lamenting spirits,
  Singing threnodes of regret.
Manhood then rebels, defiant;
  Shuts the heart and veils the eyes,
But soon trembles, fearing, grieving,
  As the dread ghosts stronger rise.

Aged hearts ?   How are they haunted ?
  Ah, by visions of the past !
By the restless thoughts of present,
  By a hand descending fast,
By the world of spirits round them,
  Which they feel, but cannot see,
By the fear to trust the slumber
  Which will take them there to be.

Be Sunny.

Does the world seem void of beauty ?
　Does your home with shade abound ?
Then this is your binding duty :
　Be the brightest thing around.

The Brook and the Wind.

Said the brook to the wind,
  " Do you not envy me,
As I flow to the ocean,
  So merry and free ?
I'm as gay as the birds
  That fly over my head.
The sky is my covering,
  The earth is my bed.

" And people, when passing,
  Will often draw near,
To hear my sweet voice
  So ringing and clear ;
And wish that they too
  Were so happy and free.
Ho, loud, harsh-voiced wind,
  Do you not envy me ? "

The wind loudly whistled,
  And said, " My dear friend,
Why you I should envy
  I don't comprehend.
You run to the ocean
  Confined in a bowl,
While I've the great world
  Beneath my control.

" ' Tis true that your voice
 Is ringing and clear,
But no one can hear you
 Unless he draws near.
My breath moves the world,
 I am free, I am wild.
Pray, why should I envy
 You, Brook, simple child ?''

There was silence a moment,
 As over the world
Queen Night her damp mantle
 Of darkness unfurled.
The heavens were darkened,
 The stars forth did peep ;
Then, the brook and the wind
 Sang each other to sleep.

Ambition's Hill.

Impatient soul, on yonder height
   Thy airy castle stands ;
Around it floats a dazzling light,
   Within are fairy bands.
The way is long and drear, I know,
   But fame and wealth are there ;
Come, gird thy armor on and go,
   And gain thy castle fair.

Why linger in the vale and sigh?
   Others have reached the goal.
Come, lay thy fears aside and fly ;
   Haste thee, thou trembling soul !
This lowly vale hath nothing grand,
   And little great or new ;
But toil and reach the airy land,
   And find a glorious view.

Thou seest the storm-cloud brooding o'er,
   Thou tremblest at the sight ;
Thou hear'st the latent thunder roar,
   Seest thou the stars of light?
Then know that he who climbs the hill,
   And conquers in the fight,
And journeys near the storm-clouds will
   Be nearer stars of light.

Courage, my soul !   Ascend the hill.
  Bravo !   You're on the track.
Let thirst for fame thy being thrill,
  And do not turn thee back.
Faster, O fast, impatient soul !
  Thy castle gleams afar !
Nearer, ah nearer, to the goal.
  Follow the guiding star !

The storms roar, the lightning gleams,
  The way is dark and long ;
Dreary the toilsome journey seems ;
  O soul, be very strong.
Onward, heed not the chasms deep ;
  Surmount them, soul, be brave ;
And journey on while thousands sleep
  And thousand others rave.

Hurrah !   A light above the world
  Dawns for thy waiting soul ;
Dispelled are clouds and storms and night,
  For thou hast reached thy goal.
The weary way thou hast o'ercome,
  Now gaze adown the vale ;
Around thee fame and praises hum,
  But hear thy followers wail.

Come, rest thee in thy castle fair ;
　Let weapons round thee fly.
Look calmly on, thy home is rare,
　Thy resting-place is high.
Thou gazest down the weary way ;
　Adown Ambition's hill.
Ah, soul, why dost thou gaze and say,
　" I'm discontented still "?

Gloomy.

Everything looks wrong to-day !
I am cross-eyed in a way !
Nothing proper is at all !
A parhelion is Old Sol !

Opportunity.

Do you see that butterfly?
Catch it, grasp it, while 'tis nigh.

A Memory.

The night is lone and drear,
  The fierce wind whistles shrill ;
At every rustle that I hear
  With fear my pulses thrill.

A form from out the past
  Before me smiling stands ;
With longing gaze she holds me fast,
  And beckons with her hands.

"Fiend!" I cry. "Why raise again
  The dreams I had forgot ?
Why waken joy and grief and pain ?
  Depart! Torment me not !

"Nay, I'll not go forth with thee.
  Back to thy resting-place !
Ah, haunting memory, let me be !
  Go, hide from me thy face.

"Back to thy weeping willows go,
  With all thy secrets hence ;
Haste to thy grave, there lay thee low,
  And rest in permanence.

"But stay! O lovely child,
    I cannot let thee go;
Stay with me, for the night is wild,
    Hark, how the rough winds blow!

"Bide with me through the lonely night,
    Stay while the mad winds rave;
But when appears the morning light
    I'll scourge thee to thy grave."

Trials.

Sweet is the song
 The Christian sings:
" Trials are shadows
 Of angels' wings."

Reflections.

PART I.

" There is no God," the scoffer says,
  " No God, no hell, no heaven ;
Worthless, unnumbered are our days,
  No Christ the world was given.

" Earth came by chance, and all
  Within it is a breath ;
We come, we live here, then we fall,
  The end of us is death.

" Nothing is lasting, good or ill ;
  Who ever saw a soul ?
The earth exists, it always will ;
  For e'er the years will roll.

" We are. I grant 'tis best to live
  A moral life ; and then
Through life, in death, we will receive
  Favor from fellow-men.

" Live well, 'tis best; then bravely die,
   Nor superstitious seem.
Whether we smile or deeply sigh,
   This life is but a dream.

" We scorn the superstitious ones
   Of many years agone,
Years hence, when ashes are our bones,
   Our children men are grown;

"Our wild beliefs, our thoughts of heaven,
   Of God, of Christ, of soul—
The same derision will be given,
   Still on the years will roll.

" Then throw the word called God away,
   Untrue its writers, preachers;
Be honest, moral, but be gay,
   Earth is the best of teachers.

" If one should ask who rules our earth,
   And whence this power so broad;
Then turn and ask him in your mirth,
   ' Whence came the wondrous God ? '

" An instant, just, from life to death;
   Creation is a dream.
Live on, be moral, yield your breath,
   Nor superstitious seem."

PART II.

" There is a God," the Christian says,
" A God eternal, true ;
Who knows our thoughts, numbers our days,
Who cares for me and you.

" Who made the earth, created all
Within it by a breath ;
Who placed us here, we cannot fall
Into eternal death.

" Death is a bridge, and when we stand
Upon it we may trust
In God to guide us by his hand,
He promised, and he must.

" I trust in God, and peace I find ;
A Saviour died for me.
I groped in darkness, I was blind ;
Christ came, and now I see.

" And yet sometimes I doubt, I feel
My own foundation fall ;
'Mid surging passions now I reel,
Yet God is all in all.

" I pray, and Jesus can becalm
A troubled soul at will ;
He with me, I can see no harm ;
He speaks, and all is still.

"I know the Word of God is good,
   It satisfies my soul.
It has for years, for ages, stood ;
   Will stand while ages roll.

"There is a power, mighty, broad ;
   This scoffers will allow.
But whence this wondrous power of God
   We cannot answer now.

"Nor should we seek to know our God.
   A heathen's god is slim ;
If we could understand our God
   We could not worship him.

"Let scoffers laugh, I'll trust in God.
   He is my help, my guide ;
I'm safe above, beneath the sod,
   A Christ for me has died."

Listen.

When you know not what to do,
   When you're tempted, faint, and weak,
Fall upon your knees and listen,
   Listen, listen, God will speak.

He will give you rest and quiet,
   He will make your heart rejoice;
When you're weak and heavy-laden,
   Listen for the Heavenly Voice.

In the Moonlight.

The day now is ending,
The dew is descending,
The shadows are flitting,
   Swift to and fro :
While above I see faintly,
Soft, downy clouds quaintly
Roll in masses as fair
   And as pure as the snow.

In the moonlight I'm sitting,
My thoughts backward flitting
To the days of my childhood,
   How quickly they fled !
Like the shadows around me
They passed, then youth found me ;
Joyous youth, bright it seemed,
   Like the moon overhead.

Now with me it travels,
No secret unravels ;
What lies in my future,
   Of woe or of weal,
Whether full of earth's treasures,
Of sorrow or pleasures,
The pathway before me,
   It cannot reveal.

A phantom appeareth!
Ah, see, now it neareth!
"Speak, speak, brilliant spirit,
    And tell me your name."
" My name is Ambition,
And from your position
I gladly will lead you
    To highways of fame.

" Fame's path is before you,
Its riches tower o'er you,
In wealth and in greatness
    Your life may abound.
O come, let me lead you,
On praise I will feed you,
With chant of your genius
    The world shall resound."

Now another ghost stealeth,
And quietly kneeleth
Before me, and bids me
    Attention to give.
" O trust me," she pleadeth,
" It is I your life needeth,
To guide you and cheer you
    While striving you live.

" Bid Ambition leave you,
She only would grieve you.
Be content, and seek not
    To be great, just be good.
The massive trees charm thee,
And almost alarm thee ;
But the sweetness of flowers
    Tells their own neighborhood."

Her voice sweetly trembled,
Ambition dissembled ;
Ambition and Lowliness
    Cannot agree.
But Lowliness cheered me,
And till slumber neared me
Her wise words of sweetness
    She whispered to me.

Anon they are flitting,
When idly I'm sitting.
Lowliness will kneel humbly,
    Ambition will tower
With visions of splendor ;
Lowliness whispers tender,
" 'Tis sweetness, not greatness,
    The charm of the flower."

Step by Step.

Suppose a man should wish to cross
    A stream, and in his pride
Should with one frantic leap attempt
    To reach the other side ;
Suppose he did this foolish act,
    When stepping stones were nigh ;
He then would meet his just reward
    If he should sink and die.

Suppose a man should with a leap,
    While standing on low ground,
Attempt to reach on ladder tall
    The very highest round.
Suppose—suppose—why, I will speak
    The truth without deduction :
He'd surely fall, and break his neck,
    And merit his destruction.

A Dialogue.

"Good morning, sir, to you.
　Pray, why are you keeping
Such early hours, sir ?
　And why are you weeping ?

"Pray tell me, kind sir,
　Why roaming these hours ?
And why do you gather
　So many wild flowers ?"

"Ah, madam, my neighbor,
　Who of all was the best,
Kind, good, and obliging,
　Has gone to his rest.

"His death was so sudden,
　In peace now he's sleeping.
I loved my good neighbor,
　That's why I am weeping."

"Dry your eyes, my good man.
　I am sure you can find
Other neighbors as honest
　As he was, and kind."

"No, ma'am. Such a neighbor
   Is not to be found,
Should I search till I died
   This wide world around."

"Tell me, sir, did you ever,
   While your neighbor was living,
Gather flowers for him, as
   To him dead you are giving?

"'You loved him,' you say;
   'He was good,' you have said.
Did you say to him living
   What you say of him dead?

"You answer not. Ah,
   More bitter you weep.
Your neighbor knows not,
   From earth he's asleep.

"Grieve on, cease not weeping;
   Pluck flowers while you may;
Talk on, spend your praises
   On a body of clay.

"But if you had given
   The half of such praise
While he lived, 'twould have cheered him,
   Like sunbeams' bright rays.

" You say I am cruel
    Thus harshly to speak ;
Well, maybe I am,
    But my comfort is weak.

" No tear-drop of sorrow
    Can I weep for you ;
But the words which I speak
    You acknowledge are true.

" Hear me now ere I leave you,
    To pass on my way :
Gather flowers for the living,
    And do not, I pray,

" Wait till your good neighbors
    Are gone to their graves,
To pass o'er their failures,
    Their virtues to praise."

.

To the Flowers.

Sweet flowers, whene'er I see you,
It seems, I know not why,
That you are heavenly footprints
Of angels passing by.

To the Stars.

Supermundane
  Gems on high,
You are jewels
  Of the sky.

King Sunshine's Choice.

"I will choose me a bride," said King Sunshine,
  "A dainty young bride from the flowers,
To partake of my joys and my pleasures,
  And to cheer me in lonelier hours.

" But my bride must be smiling and fragrant,
  And youthful and gentle and fair,
Be refined, unassuming, and healthful,
  With beauty both restful and rare."

" Then choose me," cried the rose. "I am
        fragrant,
  Your bride I right gladly would be."
" Though you're lovely and sweet," said King
        Sunshine,
  "Your boldness unfits you for me."

Then the lily, the sweet, stately lily,
  Bowed low, and with eagerness cried,
" See me, am I not fair and lovely ?
  Choose me, glowing king, for your bride."

A dark frown for an instant o'ershadowed
  The face of King Sunshine serene,
Then he answered, " By no means, proud lily,
  Would I make you my bride and my queen."

"Good King Sunshine, see me," cried a pansy.
  "Is not my face lovely and sweet ?
Should you choose me your queen and flower-bride
  Your life would be truly complete."

With a smile then King Sunshine made answer,
  "Though your face is as bright as a star,
And your ways are both gentle and winning,
  You are too gaily colored by far."

"See me," sighed the daisy.   "I'm modest,
  Your bride I am longing to be."
"Silence, daisy ; you're both rude and rustic,
  And much too uncultured for me."

Then a voice low and pleadingly whispered,
  And looking down, quite at his feet,
The great king saw a dear little violet,
  Half-calling in tones faint and sweet.

"Dainty fairy," he said, "you are pretty,
  And yet you are slender and small ;
So, you see, for a bride to King Sunshine
  You are not adapted at all."

Then the king, who was thus vainly seeking
  A bride suited just to his taste,
Saw beneath a scant covert of green leaves
  A beautiful, smiling, sweet face.

Not a word said this modest pink flower,
    But the king knew by instinct her name ;
And she trembled in joy and confusion
    At hearing him gently exclaim :

"Ah, beauties, you cannot escape me,
    I see you there hiding so low,
And I choose you my bride."   So we call her
    Arbutus—ah, beauties—you know.

Her Bridal Veil.

In a castle of old England
   Lived a maiden young and fair,
With a face of wondrous beauty
   Crowned with curls of golden hair.
And her heart was pure and guileless,
   Like the beauty of her face ;
Sweeter maid was ne'er created
   Than Lord Erskine's daughter Grace.

Poor but proud was Rupert Erskine,
   Of a grand and noble name.
A rich husband for his daughter
   Was his first and highest aim.
But Grace loved a humble artist,
   And his image filled her heart.
He was poor in worldly riches,
   Yet would give his life for art.

" Grace, my child, come here a moment,
   I have something I would say,"
Called Lord Erskine to his daughter,
   One morn in the month of May.
Quickly from among the flowers,
   With a smile upon her face,
And with both hands full of roses,
   Came his lovely daughter Grace.

Said the stern voice of her father,
   "Grace, I have a letter here
From Sir Henry True; he wants you
   To become his wife, my dear.
He is wealthy, he is famous,
   And an artist of degree.
I would choose him from all others;
  * Sure your answer yes will be."

"It is no. I do not love him,
   And my heart is not my own ;
I have given it to Arthur,
   Poor, unknown, brave Arthur Rhone.
He too is a skilful artist,
   And he is a noble man.
I have something I would ask you,
   Father, listen to my plan.

"Tell them both to paint a picture,
   Bid them choose their own design ;
Tell them it is I desire it,
   Tell them that the plan is mine.
And that he whose painted picture
   Will but suit my father's taste,
He shall have as prize of merit
   Even me, your daughter Grace

How he laughed, her haughty father.
   "Let him paint for very life,
He can ne'er produce a picture
   Which could win you for his wife."
But his angry look soon vanished,
   As amusement took its place.
And he said, "As you desire it,
   I will grant you this thing, Grace."

This consent, so quickly given,
   Made the daughter's heart rejoice,
For she knew her noble father
   Would with fairness make his choice.
Back she went among the flowers,
   With a heart quite gay and light,
Surely birds ne'er sang so sweetly,
   And the sun ne'er shone so bright.

How they worked, those two young artists!
   Each desired to do his best.
Their designs at last were chosen,
   All their skill put to the test.
And the prize, it spurred them onward,
   The reward was one for life.
And they each loved sweet Grace dearly,
   Each desired her for his wife.

Rupert Erskine's house was crowded
    When the test at last was tried ;
People wondered at this contest
    For a fair and beauteous bride.
Great indeed the consternation,
    For the earl was known to fame ;
People wondered, people questioned,
    What on earth could be his aim.

First Sir Henry brought his picture ;
    Every one it seemed to suit,
It was rarely rich and perfect,
    'Twas of autumn-tinted fruit.
As they gazed, the birds drew near it,
    Feeling naught of natural fright,
And Lord Erskine was enraptured
    At that perfect painted sight.

Surely this would win his daughter ;
    Arthur Rhone could never make
View like this, so grand, so perfect ;
    Surely this the prize would take.
As for Grace, she calmly waited,
    Did not doubt young Arthur's skill ;
To the breathless praise she listened,
    Listened, hoping, praying still.

There was silence for a moment;
   Arthur Rhone came through the crowd,
In his arms he bore a picture,
   To the earl he lowly bowed.
" Here," exclaimed the earl in anger,
   " Take the veil from off your view!"
" Nay, my lord," the artist answered;
   " I shall leave that work for you."

The earl frowned, tried to remove it.
   " Well, by all the stars that shine,
'Tis a painted veil, 'tis perfect,
   Looks like silk, of texture fine ! "
And the people did not wonder,
   When he said, " This suits my taste.
You have won her fairly, bravely;
   You may have my daughter Grace."

Said young Arthur, freely, kindly,
   As he took Lord Erskine's hand,
" I have won the fairest lady
   To be found in all our land."
Henry True now greeted Arthur,
   As his manly cheek grew pale,
" You deserve your bride, my brother,
   You designed her bridal veil."

A Tree and a Flower.

(What the tree said :)

    " To bear the wind and rain and sleet,
       And wintry blasts, I'm fated ;
    To many blows I am exposed
       Because I'm elevated."

    A flower, nestling at his feet,
       Could hear the monarch grumble,
    And whispered low, in sweet content,
       "I'm safe because I'm humble."

Autumn.

Who that incendiary
  That sets the forests burning?
Fair Summer, bowing, answered low,
  " My brother is returning."

King Winter.

The Autumn wailed, "I felt his breath."
   The birds departed, frightened.
The heavens frowned, and all the earth
   In chilling terror whitened.

The flowers clasped his frozen hands,
   And bended low to greet him ;
The leaves, all clad in colors gay,
   Then sallied forth to meet him.

King Winter came, but gave the earth
   A coldly warm protection ;
Till Spring commanded, " Rise, depart;
   I am the resurrection."

The Seasons.

'Tis Autumn; the forests are burning with beauty.
A veil of gay figures is over our land,
Which soon must be lifted, O beautiful Autumn,
True symbol of life here, so fleeting, so grand.

A wailing is heard through the mountains and
valleys,
'Tis Winter, the flowers bend low at his breath;
His cold hand descendeth, his presence appeareth,
O cruel, cold Winter, pure symbol of death.

The sunlight appeareth, cold Winter is yielding,
Wings rush overhead, sweet bird-voices sing.
The flowers all rise. Of the glad resurrection
Is Spring a true symbol, the life-giving Spring.

More sunlight, more music, more fathomless glory,
More life and more flowers and more to unfold;
If to us is given a symbol of heaven,
'Tis Summer, whose beauties can never be told.

Death.

He surely will come,
   Your soul is his prize ;
He's coming to take it,
   So just close your eyes.

And yet do not fear.
   He is gentle, is death ;
All he asks you to do
   Is to give him your breath.

And then he will take you
   To the home you have made ;
So just close your eyes,
   And don't be afraid.

To a Bereaved One.

And is your loved one resting?
  And do you almost fear
Your heart will break with sorrow?
  Why should I try to cheer?

Ah, weak indeed the comfort
  Which my poor wisdom gives;
I'll simply beckon you to heaven,
  For there thy dear one lives.

Dreams.

Weary of your life, you say?
  Dark your pathway seems?
Once your life was glad and gay!
  Then thank God for dreams.

The Fern.

Violets and fairy mayflowers,
    Buttercups and daisies too,
Roses, lilies, clover, pansies,
    All are magical, 'tis true.
But my choice in the botanic
    Is a species never tall,
Grows in humid soil, is verdant,
    But is not a flower at all.

'Tis not popular nor petted,
    Is not beautiful nor coy ;
Yet consider it, and you will
    All these adjectives employ—
Dainty, gentle, restful, winning,
    Balmy, comely, fresh, and sweet ;
Gifted with the grace of fairies
    And with symmetry complete ;

Never haughty nor disdainful,
    But of graceful, modest mien ;
Not high-colored, but contented
    With a dress of simple green.
Though not loved by all or many,
    Yet to me it is the best ;
For to see it is refreshing,
    In its presence there is rest.

In the forest you may find it,
  You may find it in the dale,
And when lonely sit beside it
  And contentment you'll inhale ;
For its balm then do I love it,
  And this lesson true I learn,
There is rest and sweet enchantment
  In the shadow of a fern.

The Wood-nymph's Song.

In the early hours of morning,
    When the flowers are all asleep,
While the moon, though very faintly,
    Doth her watch o'er slumber keep;
While the grass with dew is sparkling,
    And the bees and birds are still,
Then I love to roam the forests,
    Love to wander at my will.

When the sun, high in the heavens,
    Gold is throwing everywhere,
While the flowers their bells are ringing
    In the balmy, scented air ;
While the birds their songs are singing,
    Which to charm me never fail,
Then I love to roam the forests,
    Nature's beauty to inhale.

In the evening, in the twilight,
    When the birds to rest have gone,
When the nightly dew is falling,
    And the world seems sad and lone;
When the only singer near me
    Is the noisy whippoorwill,
Then I love to roam the forests,
    And to wander where I will.

In the solemn hours of midnight,
   When the flowers are all asleep,
While the moon in all her radiance
   Doth her ceaseless vigil keep ;
When I too am lost in slumber,
   Knowing not what Nature tells,
Then I love to roam in dreamland,
   Through the forest's woody dells..

The Three Wishes.

"If I should see a fairy, mamma,
   And it should speak to me,
And would give me what I wanted,
   Whatever it might be,
I'd surely ask for wealth, dear mamma,
   That I might dress so fine ;
With wealth, position high, and jewels,
   A happy life be mine."

"What would you ask for, sister,
   Should you the fairy see,
And it gave the same privilege
   To you as well as me ? "
"I should ask for beauty, Gracie,
   Such as was never seen,
More lovely than a butterfly,
   More graceful than a queen."

"And now," said little Ida,
   The youngest of the three,
" I'll tell what I would ask for,
   Should I the fairy see—
I would ask for faith and love
   To believe on Jesus' name ;
I ask not treasures of this world,
   Beyond them is my aim."

" My children," said the mother,
   " Your sister asks the best.
No wealth or beauty can e'er equal
   Love, hope, and heavenly rest ;
The wish of Ida is to be
   Safe in the peaceful fold,
And this is better, better far,
   Than beauty, silver, or gold."

Some Say.

Some say that love is like the rain,
  Which falls until the leaves
And every object round about
  A beauty new receives;
That, if the rain is absent long,
  The leaves will droop to die,
For nothing but another shower
  Their thirst can satisfy.

Some say that love is like a vine,
  Which lives, and grows, and clings,
And reaches out its tendrils fine,
  Embracing many things.
Then if perchance an object falls,
  About which it has twined,
It still will seek, and reach, and long
  Another one to find.

Some say that love is like the sun,
  Which bursts the clouds apart,
And finds the morning-glory closed,
  But pierces to her heart,
Until her face is all aglow
  With sunshine warm and bright;
When in an ecstasy complete
  She hides her face in fright.

If any one should come to me,
   'To ask me which was right—
Whether true love was like the rain,
   Or vine, or sunshine bright—
I'm sure I would not answer,
   For my heart withholds its story,
But, somehow, I would rather be
   Loved like the morning-glory.

A Few Wild Flowers.

Once some tiny rustic flowers
   Grew in humid, verdant soil,
Envied not blooms cultivated,
   Knew not weariness or toil.

Held the sunshine in the daytime,
   In the evening held the dew ;
Happily they gaily danced to
   Every tune the breezes blew.

As I spied them how they trembled,
   Quickly bending low they lay ;
Then with happy tears their faces
   Sparkled as I went away.

When I turned and gently plucked them,
   How their faces pallid grew !
To a sick friend then I gave them,
   Much she praised their dainty hue,

Praised their fragrance and their sweetness,
   And their beauty, rustic, rare ;
Then I placed them by her bedside,
   Watered, tended them with care.

Soon I took them, damp and dripping,
    From their place beside her bed,
And arranged and placed them gently
    In the fingers of the dead.

As I bended o'er my dear friend,
    Pressed a kiss on her cold cheek,
And beheld the flowers held closely,
    In my mind thus did I speak :

"Sweet love's tokens, gifts from heaven,
    You have soothed and eased her pain,
You have cheered a heart one moment,
    So you have not lived in vain,
With her you have crossed death's portal,
    And in heaven you'll bloom again."

Sin.

A rose there grew, all white and sweet,
  Its spotless beauty was complete.
An insect came, and in a day
  Took perfect purity away.

Who Doubts?

Who doubts the world exists ?
  Who doubts that it revolves ?
Who doubts the shining of the sun ?
  But who the mystery solves ?

Who doubts the stars and planets are ?
  Who doubts that breezes sigh ?
Who says there are no clouds or storms ?
  Who never saw the sky ?

Who says that he has walked on earth
  And never touched the sod ?
Who lives, and breathes, and feels, and yet
  Can disbelieve his God ?

Life's Morning and Evening.

Morning.

Sparkling faces, merry hearts,
　　Gaily ringing voices,
Singing songs of sweetness till
　　Many a soul rejoices.

Evening.

Placid faces, happy hearts,
　　Voices low and tender,
Breathing words which jewels are
　　In a crown of splendor.

A Lesson from the Flowers.

I was sitting in a forest,
    Underneath a spreading tree.
Golden sunbeams, bright and cheery,
    Freely gave their life to me.
Breezes gently fanned my forehead,
    All around was sweet and gay,
Yet in spite of Nature's brightness,
    I was sad this happy day.

Thoughtful was I ; o'er me feelings
    Rushed with misery intense.
What is life?   Ah, all around me
    Is but mystery all dense.
With a veil is heaven hidden,
    Earth is dreary and forlorn ;
Better had no life been given,
    Better had I ne'er been born.

By my side some tiny flowers,
    Violets all pure and white,
Filled the air with sweetest perfume,
    Welcome were they to my sight.
" Sweetest flowers which bloom," I whispered,
    " Fairy forms with angel's breath,
Are you glad that you are living?
    Are you not afraid of death?"

Suddenly the gentlest music,
 As of ringing silver bells,
Filled the air with sweetest accents,
 Echoed through those woody dells.
"We have listened," said the violets,
 "To your sad, complaining voice,
While around, the sun, the breezes,
 And the birds all cried, 'Rejoice!'

"You have praised our breath of sweetness,
 You are glad that we abound,
Yet our fragrance ne'er had cheered you
 Had we stayed beneath the ground;
Had we hidden from God's sunlight
 We would ne'er had life to give.
Darkness bound us, light has found us,
 'Tis for others that we live.

"Death we fear not, Christ has risen,
 Even so do we arise.
Every day our life goes floating
 Onward, upward, to the skies.
Listen to us while the secret
 Of the flowers we now unroll;
We, like you, are made immortal,
 And our fragrance is our soul."

Suddenly the sun shone brightly,
   Suddenly the world seemed fair,
Bird-songs seemed like angel's music,
   Beauties floated in the air.
"Angel messengers," I whispered,
   " You have taught me how to live ;
Life is given me for others,
   Life is given me to give."

The Mountain Breeze and the Ocean Breeze.

"Happy am I," said the breeze of the mountain,
As it saluted the breeze of the sea,
"Happy am I, o'er the mountains I whisper,
Whistling as gay as the birds in my glee.

"Noble old mountains, like arms they encircle,
Sweet benedictions they seem to let fall,
Showering their blessings on those in the valley,
Guarding, protecting, and caring for all.

"Glorious old mountains, they tell of God's glory.
Small seems the earth ; O, my life is so free !
Happy am I, the breeze of the mountain.
Are you so happy, sweet breeze of the sea?"

Sweetly this answer the ocean breeze whispered:
"Happy, O perfectly happy, am I.
Though no grand mountains I have to inspire me,
Above and around me I see the blue sky.

"Earth seems so great to me, breeze of the moun-
tain,
Stretching far out, out away from my sight ;
Then the old ocean forever inspires me.
Happy am I ; O, my life is so bright.

" Heaven, like a tent, seems to guard and protect
      ·me,
Ocean around me and heaven above,
Happy am I, in a tent of God's mercy,
   Guarded by heaven and filled with his love.''

Sweetly then whispered the breezes together,
   '' Happiness fills us wherever we live ;
God gives his life to us, freely, abundantly,
   This life we love to his creatures to give.

'' Mountains and oceans all tell of his greatness,
   Heaven and earth join his love to proclaim.
Praise him, ye nations !   Ye angels, adore him !
   Infinite greatness and love is his name.''

Tiresome Sometimes.

Nature, towering, proudly asked,
"Do you not admire me?"
"Hush," I cried, "you know I do,
But just now you tire me."

The March Wind.

Hear the March wind, like a monarch it passes ;
   See the great trees in humility bend.
Shrill is the voice ; of sorrow or gladness,
   What is the message it brings you, my friend?

Is the March wind to you rough or forbidding?
   Is it a voice of hate or of love?
Does it lament with you over your sorrow?
   Or does it call you to mansions above?

Does it e'er seem that the wind is the wailing
   Of the lost spirits departed from earth?
Or does it seem as the cruel rejoicing
 . Of the glad demons all screaming with mirth?

Sometimes it seems, when the fierce winds are
      calling,
   That 'tis the voice of the poor soulless trees,
Calling to heaven for a soul to enliven,
   And make them forever as free as the breeze.

Sometimes the wind seems the voice of ambition,
   Calling me up to my visions of joy,
Bidding me climb to my brilliant air-castles,
   Where no ill winds can ever annoy.

Sometimes it seems like a fierce rushing army,
  Sometimes it seems like the spirit of God ;
Sometimes it seems like the archangel's trumpet
  Calling the flowers to rise from the sod.

Many and sweet are the fierce March wind lessons ;
  Each soul translates in a different voice ;
Nature alone has the key-note of meaning.
  Free as the wind let us rise and rejoice.

The Advent of Music.

Come with me to Eden's garden,
　To the time when Adam first
Tasted the forbidden apple,
　Making all the world accursed.
Suddenly a darkness gath'ring
　Shades the beauteous garden now.
And a voice is sternly asking,
　"Adam, Adam, where art thou?

" Not as usual dost thou hasten
　My approval to obtain ;
Hast thou gratified the passion
　That I warned thee to restrain?
Hast thou tasted of the apple?
　Didst thou not my word believe?
Hither, Adam, from thy arbor,
　And thy sentence now receive."

Then together from their covert,
　Eve and Adam, hand in hand,
Guiltily approach their Maker,
　And before him silent stand.
Waiting to receive his judgment,
　God their inmost thoughts can read.
Sternly, pityingly spake he :
　" Guilty art thou, man, indeed.

"Guilty art thou, first of women,
　　Guilty, there is no reprieve;
For thy crime all earth henceforward
　　Sin and death must e'er receive.
All divine and heavenly beauties
　　Which I placed on earth for thee
Must to heaven be now transported,
　　Never more on earth to be."

"Nay, not so," cried guilty Adam.
　　"Let one gift from thee be given,
To make earth divine, to cause men
　　To love beauty, to love heaven.
Grant my prayer, O just Creator,
　　But one gift from heaven above,
But one gift from God to mortals,
　　As a proof of heavenly love."

Sweetly spoke our great Creator,
　　"Adam, I will grant thy prayer;
I from heaven will send a token
　　Which will lighten all your care;
Which will fill all heaven with sweetness,
　　When all things from earth have passed;
Which will purify your being;
　　Which eternally shall last."

As he spoke, a gentle murmur
  Sweetly trembled everywhere.
Divine music filled all nature,
  Filled the heavens, filled the air ;
Thrilled the soul of Eve, of Adam,
  Filled the heart of every bird ;
Filled the brooks and filled the breezes.
  Music everywhere was heard.

Music then was God's great token,
  Music was the gift he gave,
Telling of his love and pardon,
  Telling of his power to save.
Music share we with the angels,
  And, when all from earth is passed,
Music only of earth's blessings
  Through eternity shall last.

Setting Sun.

The sun departed, blushing
   At the crimes he had unfurled.
I should think, as old as Sun is,
   He would understand the world.

Growth in Heaven.

There came a soul to earth,
  A mother's heart was cheered ;
Earth seemed to gain new beauty,
  And brighter life appeared.

The soul was called to heaven,
  Earth tried its flight to stay ;
God whispered gently, firmly,
  "I give, I take away."

A mother's heart was broken,
  Earth lost for her its light.
Her child, her life, her darling,
  Was taken from her sight.

"Come back, my child," she whispered,
  It seemed the child-soul heard,
The mother breathless listened,
  And caught a whispered word—

"I dwell in fairer places,
  And heavenly sights I see.
I cannot come to you again,
  But you may come to me."

That loving, distant echo,
  Those words so sweet and mild,
Fell softly on the mother's heart,
  And she was reconciled.

A moment's time was over,
    And life through death was given.
The mother left the friends of earth
    To meet the child in heaven.

" Where is my child? " she questioned.
    A form of beauty mild
Approached her, then these words of love,
    " Mother, I am your child."

The mother gazed in wonder,
    Heard she her own child speak?
Was this youth, noble, manly,
    Her babe so helpless, weak?

The mother heart then understood
    That God's way was the best.
She found her child as sweet and pure
    As when he left her breast.

Her child had dwelt in innocence,
    Earth's paths had never trod ;
Had thriven in light celestial,
    E'en in the light of God.

Thrice happy child who early leaves,
    With wings unsoiled and white,
Earth's ways of sorrow, grief, and sin,
    To dwell in heavenly light.

Satan.

Satan is a spider,
  A crawling, base deceiver,
Whose web cannot be copied
  By any other weaver;
And woe be to the little fly
  Who by him is allured,
For a fly once spider-bitten
  Is never wholly cured.

Why?

The birds sing when they greet me,
  The flowers lowly bow,
The sun smiles upon me,
  The breezes fan my brow.

The butterfly comes dancing,
  And from the forest still
I hear a gentle murmur,
  The singing of the rill.

When all these pretty people
  Greet me, and love me so,
Why is my heart so sorrowful?
  Does anybody know?

Just a Cabin.

Just a humble little cottage,
   Left to ruin and decay ;
Just a lonely hut, forsaken,
   Witness of a better day.
Shattered, tumbled-down, and homely,
   Just a wreck about to fall,
Stands serenely by the roadside,
   Just a ruin, that is all.

It may be some one is dreaming
   Of that wretched little place ;
It may be a tear of sorrow
   Stains a sad and thoughtful face.
It may be in some strange country,
   Orphaned, friendless, and alone,
Some one dreams of that poor cottage,
   Whispering softly, "Home, sweet home."

Ah, that cabin stands before us,
   Yet we know not what it means.
We can see the stage forsaken,
   Past, unknown to us the scenes.
Then we'll pass the cabin gently,
   As it stands before us lone,
Years ago this humble dwelling
   Bore the honored name of "home."

Sweet Home.

O that I might write a poem
Of a sweet and rural valley,
Where there stands a rustic cabin
   Which was once sweet home to me.
There the flowers are ever blooming,
There the evergreen entwineth,
There the blithesome birds are singing,
   There I lived content and free.

Let me paint for you a picture
Of my Eden in this valley.
Just a humble, rude log cabin
   Covered o'er with flowers and vines.
On the right a clump of thickets
Where the frisky squirrels sported ;
On the left a shady arbor,
   Formed by massive, towering pines.

Near the house, quite close beside it,
Was a well, with curb moss-covered ;
Near it was the oaken bucket,
   Leaning on it was the sweep ;
Standing near the well, o'erbending,
Was a maple tree gigantic,
Whose immense, outspreading branches
   Seemed majestic watch to keep.

Just behind the cot a river
Danced and rippled in the sunlight,
Where the fishes, unmolested,
    Swam in happiness content.
Near the bank a sturdy shade-tree
Stood.   Its limbs a seat afforded,
There in peace with book or pencil
    Many quiet hours I've spent.

Come with me across the river,
See the green and verdant meadow ;
Here the birds and bees delighted,
    Here the sweet wild flowers grew.
Here the violets, fair beauties,
Shed their fragrance on the air,
Here the daisies and the lilies
    Sported while the breezes blew.

Linger with me here till sunset
Tints the western sky with beauty.
O behold the gold and crimson!
    Is it not a glorious sight ?
Seems as if ten thousand ribbons
Waved in freedom there to cheer us,
And there reaches to the river,
    As it seems, a path of light.

O what beauty !   O what glory !
O that I might write a poem
Which would all the hidden meaning
   Of this scene to you reveal.
But they tell me a true poem
Is a thought, and not a metre,
So perchance you can imagine
   What I must perforce conceal.

Noisy city, cease your riot.
Let me wander back in thoughtland,
Let me through the veil of dreaming
   See that cabin by the lea.
In your realm, Imagination,
Let me be again an inmate
Of that rude and rough log cabin
   Which was once " sweet home " to me.

Weavers.

In the shadow, calmly weaving,
  Sat a woman old and gray.
In her web a square was fashioned,
  True, her pattern was not gay,
Yet the scenes her spirit cherished
  In her web were woven there;
No one knew except the weaver
  Why her pattern was a square.

In the sunshine, slowly weaving
  In a web of beauty rare,
Weaving sunbeams in a circle,
  Sat a woman young and fair.
Faces greeted her, she wove them
  Firmly in her web; it crowned
Her at last, and many wondered
  How she wove her web so round.

In the gaslight, laughing, weaving,
  Lovers watching her the while,
Was a lady, gay and merry.
  Like a diamond was the style
Of her web; it brightly glistened,
  For its threads were all of gold.
Yet the pictures interwoven
  Disappeared at every fold.

In the gloaming, eager, weaving,
   Sadly smiling as she wove,
Sat a woman old and saintly.
   In her web was sweetest love,
Woven in a starlike pattern,
   Which like lances gleams afar;
No one knew except the weaver
   Why her pattern was a star.

Air-castles.

Are you building air-castles
  For your recreation?
An air-castle is good
  If it has a foundation.

But lay the foundation
  Down solid and square ;
Then build all the castles
  You want to of air.

Goldenrod.

All the roses, daisies, lilies,
　　Shivered as they saw her face ;
Clasped the hands of chilling Autumn,
　　Bended low and left the place.

But the stately, golden princess
　　Stood unmoved before the sight ;
Heeded not the wind's rough greeting,
　　Held her shining head upright.

I was passing by the wayside,
　　And I saw her standing there.
I could but admire her courage,
　　Though she was not sweet nor fair.

And I stopped and asked her, saying,
　　" Tell me, golden princess, pray,
Why you, hard and unrelenting,
　　Watch the flowers pass away.

" Why you come as death's drear symbol,
　　When of summer we're bereaved.
Tell me, if you can remember,
　　Whence your name you have received."

Proudly rose the fearless princess,
　　Rose with royal, wondrous grace ;
And she looked with gaze unflinching
　　Boldy, sadly, in my face.

Then she whispered, "Ah, you wrong me,
　　No one sorrows more than I
At the death of beauteous summer,
　　For the flowers as they die.

" Do I seem to you so hardened?
　　Am I cruel?　Am I bold?
Yet I have undaunted courage,
　　And I have a heart of gold.

" Though I am of death a symbol,
　　Let me tell you, ere we part,
That I have the summer's sunshine
　　Folded warmly to my heart.

"And I come to bring this lesson
　　From the dusty wayside sod,
Though it seems so sad and dreary,
　　Death is but a *golden rod!* "

Lady Chesby.

In her chamber sat the lady,
All unbound her raven tresses,
Which o'er white and graceful shoulders
   In their silken beauty fell;
One could see she was not happy,
And that sadness rested o'er her,
Yet but few e'er heard her story,
   Which I am about to tell.

Yet it is the same old story,
That so oft has been repeated.
In her youth a poor young lover
   Offered her his heart and hand;
And another, now her husband,
Too had sought her final answer;
And she married him for riches,
   At her father's stern command.

But to-night, alone and pensive,
Lady Chesby's thoughts turned backward.
Once again her heart grew happy,
   For she was again a child,
Walking through the scented wildwood
In the twilight dim and holy;
And she seemed to see young Harold,
   Hear his voice so low and mild,

As he said, " Though they may part us,
I still love you, Nellie darling;
You are in my heart forever,
 Will be, till my latest breath."
And she seemed to say in answer,
" Harold, though I wed another,
I shall always love you truly,
 For my love is strong as death."

Then she heard the cry of anguish,
Of the last time that she met him :
" Good-by, good-by, little Nellie,
 With you now for aye I part;
But the locket that you gave me,
With the lock of hair within it,
Rests forever, aye forever,
 Near the beating of my heart."

Interrupted was her musing
As her maid appeared before her—
" O my lady, may I tell you
 Something which occurred to-day?"
Lady Chesby smiled approval,
"Ah yes, Dorcas, you may tell me ;
I will listen with all interest
 To whate'er you have to say."

" In the hospital, my lady,
Where my sister Mary labors,
A poor stranger there was carried,
    And to-day it was he died.
But before his final summons,
Ere his life from him was taken,
He with low and feeble accents
    Called my sister to his side.

"And he told her a strange story,
How when he was gay and youthful
He had loved a fair, sweet maiden,
    Who had given him her heart.
And he had a tiny locket,
With a lock of hair within it ;
Which he said ' belonged to Nellie.'
    It was resting near his heart.

"And he said that from the hour
He had parted from the maiden
He had always worn that locket
    Near his heart, upon his breast ;
And he told her, although Nellie
Had been forced to wed another,
Still he treasured her assurance
    She would always love him best.

" That is all, dear Lady Chesby;
But why do you look so pallid ?
Are you cold ?   Why do you shiver ?
    Lady—O, what have I done ! "
" No, no, Dorcas; nothing ails me,
Only I am sad and lonely,
And your story is peculiar.
    Now I wish to be alone."

When alone she rose, and quickly
Drew a shawl around her shoulders,
And a cloak of warmth and thickness
    Folded she about her form ;
Placed a veil upon her features,
That no one might recognize her ;
Then she fearlessly and boldly,
    Resolutely, faced the storm.

Soon she knocked and was admitted
To the chamber of the stranger
Who had died that winter morning,
    Now was lying cold and dead.
Lady Chesby at once knew him
As her true rejected lover ;
And her tears they fell in torrents,
    As she knelt beside the bed.

Deftly she obtained the locket
Which was resting on his bosom;
Then again with heart of anguish
　　Homeward she her steps did turn.
Ah, the snowflakes seemed to blind her,
And the wind to blow more fiercely,
While around her, bright and mocking,
　　Did the flaring gaslights burn.

No one knew who was the lady
Who had called that winter evening,
Who, disguised, had sought admittance
　　To the chamber of the dead;
Had obtained the golden locket
That was resting on his bosom,
And had wept with better anguish
　　As she knelt beside the bed.

No one knew that Lady Chesby,
As she smiled in social circles,
Had a gnawing, bitter sorrow,
　　That she could not sleep or rest;
That her heart was bleeding, broken,
That her heart's love all was buried,
That a tiny golden locket
　　Rested gently on her breast.

People called her stately, haughty,
As she absently moved round them ;
Some said she had no emotion,
    That her heart was still and cold.
No one knew the life of Nellie,
No one understood the lady,
Not until her dying moments
    Was her bitter secret told.

Freaky.

Is Nature always smiling ?
    No, she's a freaky child ;
She will not beam upon you
    Until you first have smiled.

Easter Lily.

Years and years ago, the flowers
   Thought to choose themselves a queen—
One of sweet and stately bearing,
   One of gentle, modest mien.
All the flowers called together
   To the Saviour's garden came,
Where by his own gentle bidding
   Every bloom received its name.

Who should be the queen ?   The flowers
   Found it hard this to declare ;
Some were beautiful but haughty,
   Some were sweet but were not fair,
Some too gentle, some too slender,
   Some too gaily colored were.
But at last one cried, '' The lily,''
   All the flowers turned to her.

Then the lily rose before them,
   Tall and stately, sweet and good,
Purple, fair, the purest flower
   In the garden, lily stood.
For her manner, sweet and royal,
   For her beauty, grand and rare,
She was chosen for their queen, and
   Called '' the fairest of the fair.''

Then the lily raised her petals,
    Gone her quiet, modest mien;
And with pride her heart was swollen,
    Had she not been chosen queen?
Then in accents low and earnest
    To herself the lily said,
"To no one in earth or heaven
    Will I ever bow my head!"

In the holy hour of twilight
    Jesus to the garden went.
As the flowers felt his presence
    Every blossom lowly bent,
Held its breath and listened eager
    For his voice so low and sweet.
And the grass was proud and happy
    To be carpet for his feet.

Softly passed he by the flowers,
    Speaking gently to each one.
At his touch with bliss they trembled,
    Gleamed his beauty like the sun.
It is said one little flower
    In her joy forgot her name.
Every flower-head was bended
    As the Saviour near it came.

All but one, the queen, the lily—
　　She, the pride of all the flowers,
Haughtily, with head uplifted,
　　By the Saviour's side she towers.
Gazing proudly at his beauty,
　To herself again she said,
" To no one in earth or heaven
　　Will I ever bow my head."

Jesus knew her thoughts and loved her,
　　Jesus saw her heart of pride.
Softly came he through the garden,
　　Sadly stood he by her side,
Gazed upon her, loving, pleading,
　　While the other flowers said,
" Lily, queen, it is the Saviour ;
　　Lily, lily, bend your head."

When she knew it was the Saviour
　　Lily's cheeks were blanched with shame,
As the Saviour gazed upon her
　　Purest white her heart became.
While her soul, filled with repentance,
　　Saw the Saviour's tears of blood,
As with head now lowly bowing
　　At his blessed feet she stood.

Discontent.

I sat alone within my room.
The moonlight smiled upon the gloom ;

When entered Discontent, unbid,
And to my side by stealth he slid.

I shrank away, and called to Pride,
Then in my trembling weakness cried:

" My home is sweet, my heart is free ;
Fiend, why dost thou trouble me ? "

With scorn he glanced my treasure o'er,
And pointed at an open door.

"Go, go ! " I cried; but he, instead
Of going at my mandate, said :

"An ever present foe am I,
I'll follow you until you die."

" I will defy you," I replied,
As joyfully I followed Pride.

She led me by a gleaming way
O'er fields of light for many a day.

My travels o'er, I banished Fear,
I sat alone, I called for Cheer.

Then o'er my shoulder, mocking, leaned
A well known, hated, dreaded fiend.

I shrank away ; he rudely cried,
"Away with Cheer and Fear and Pride !

"An ever present foe am I,
I'll follow you until you die."

The Ocean's Bride.

A broad expanse of clear, dark space,
　A star-decked vault above ;
An atmosphere of silent power,
　Which thrilled my heart with love.

A splendid moon, which seemed to rise
　From heart of Ocean old,
And to my human eyes appeared
　A ball of shining gold.

Higher and higher did it rise
　Until all gleaming, bright,
It seemed to make 'twixt earth and heaven
　A shining path of light.

O Luna, bride of Ocean old,
　You light his heart of blue ;
Though you deign not to notice us,
　Yet we adore you.

We gaze upon your loveliness,
　And know that you were given
To mark for us a path of light
　And guide our thoughts to heaven.

At the Seaside.

Let artists rave, let poets sing
   The cottage by the sea.
I love the mountains. I would sing
   A cottage by the lea ;
Where brooklets bubble, flowers bloom,
   And mountains towering stand.
Serenely there King Silence reigns,
   And all is sweet and grand.

I've left you, dear old mountains,
   I'm stationed by the sea ;
And yet, though absent, you are dear,
   E'en now the theme for me.
I've learned anew this lesson true,
   That, wheresoe'er I roam,
No spot on earth is half so dear
   To me as " home, sweet home."

Vacillating.

(What I said yesterday:)

How fair the world appears!
  How bright the sunbeams shine!
How full of joy am I!
  How glad a life is mine!

(What I say to-day:)

How gloomy is the world!
  The day with storms is fed!
How sorrowful am I!
  I wish that I were dead!

The Sabbath in the Mountains.

How fair, how pure, how holy
   The sunlight doth appear ;
How faintly yet how clearly
   The song of bird I hear.
What means this holy stillness ?
   The breeze then seemed to say,
In whispers full of sweetness,
   " This is the Sabbath day."

To a Mountain Brook.

Dear little brook, what a lesson you teach me,
    As through the lone forest you merrily flow ;
Singing and sparkling and ever contented
    To make some one happy wherever you go.

Cheering the sad heart of some weary traveler,
    Many a wanderer has stood at your brink,
Where you have charmed him by smiling so
        brightly,
    To sing him a song or to give him a drink.

Calling the birds to your side by your music,
    You give them refreshment, and ask not for pay.
Dear little brook, you have set me a copy
    And taught me a lesson this fair summer day.

Daily Bread.

There! Do not look far ahead!
Calmly eat your daily bread.
Do your duty, do your best,
And trust God to do the rest.

Twilight.

When Beauty breathes her soul through Nature's
　　　own,
　　And Nature reverent is, and peaceful still,
I, sitting silent, thoughtful, and alone,
　　Feel all my soul glow with a mystic thrill.

A fervent adoration seems to steal
　　Upon my heart.　O twilight angel dear,
I pray you lift the veil which I can feel,
　　Reveal the world of spirits hovering near.

And now a whisper low and faintly seems
　　To breathe into my listening spirit's ear ;
The while I bend to catch the sunset beams,
　　This message to my waiting soul I·hear :

" Seek not to know the realm that lies beyond
　　The veil ; bright sunset clouds are now unrolled,
And all the world for you is now adorned
　　With dazzling light and splendors manifold.

" Behold the earth, divine it doth appear !
　　Ah, heaven alone is fairer ; could you see
Into the heart of this that wraps you here,
　　You'd see the soul of heaven's mystery."

Midnight

'Tis midnight ; darkness reigneth o'er the earth.
  The moon and stars like eyes of metal glare,
And seem to gaze at me with scorn intense and
        mirth.
  A sense of littleness pervades the air,

And I inhale it ; meekly, deeply I absorb
  My fill of humbleness. I am so weak and small ;
The heavens, the worlds above me, and this earthly
        orb
  Are fearful—their Creator all in all.

A breath of awfulness is in the air,
  The stillness of the world pervades my soul ;
A sense of power enthroned I know not where
  Comes o'er my senses. Life is a fearful dole.

And what am I that I should dare to doubt
  Existence of a wondrous power divine,
When I behold so much ! a power without which
  Life all void and useless would be mine.

O mighty One, whate'er, where'er thou art,
  Who madest, who rulest the wonders which I see,
I do not dare to doubt. Accept my heart,
  My soul, myself, and all I hope to be.

The Drunkard's Wife.'

A dismal scene.　A gloomy room,
　Damp, fireless, cheerless, drear ;
A dimly burning lamp, a face
　Transfixed with pain and fear ;
A story there so plainly told,
　A sad, an unloved life.
She is on earth, she is in hell,
　She is a drunkard's wife.

She shivers as she lifts her face,
　Then buries it again
Within her hands ; she sighs, she sobs
　As if with hidden pain.
O God, she cannot understand
　Why she is thus unblest ;
O why not let her die, and find
　Sweet, peaceful, needed rest ?

Again she lifts her face ; the lamp
　Still low and lower burns.
O heaven, for fire, for light, for food,
　For love her spirit yearns.
How slow the moments pass !
　And will it e'er be light ?
Hark ! the town clock sadly strikes
　The hour of midnight.

"Twelve, twelve;" no other sound she hears,
  And will her soul go wild?
Her face is hard with bitter woe,
  It once was soft and mild.
Her silvery hair, so thin and white,
  Once shone with golden gleams;
She once had happiness and home,
  Now she has only dreams.

Hark! O he comes, the drunkard comes.
  She opens wide the door;
He staggers in and falls a heap
  Incarnate on the floor.
While she resumes her weary watch
  Alone, how drear her life!
O mighty God, if thou art God,
  Help thou the drunkard's wife!

Bona and Mala.

I have two firm companions,
   And they are very queer ;
One has the name of Bona,
   And she to me is dear.

Yet oft I rudely spurn her,
   She lingeringly goes ;
And then her bitter rival
   Instantaneously knows,

And comes to vex my spirit ;
   You can surmise her name,
Mala, surnamed Pessima,
   Destruction is her aim.

These two, my strange companions,
   Can never quite agree ;
When I admit the one in heart,
   The other goes from me.

Forever they are near me,
   From morning until night.
The one pleads with me gently
   To lead me in the right ;

The other breathes upon me
  With poison in her breath,
Then brings to me forbidden fruit
  To feed me on to death.

When I look hard at Mala,
  At first she seems so bright ;
Then smaller grows, and uglier,
  Then disappears from sight.

But when I gaze at Bona,
  At first she seems so small ;
Then she larger, brighter grows,
  Till splendor gleams o'er all.

The Reason Why.

Sometimes my heart is joyful,
    The world seems gay and bright;
Man and bird and beast I love,
    Toward all my heart is right.
And really as I sing it seems
    That everything is good;
It seems I easily could preach
    A sermon, if I would.

Again my heart is dismal,
    And time seems dark and long;
Man and bird and beast I hate,
    Toward all my heart is wrong.
And as I frown it seems to me
    That everything is bad,
That I would rid myself of life
    If God's permit I had.

I'll tell you why I flitter
    From righteousness to evil—
Sometimes I entertain the Lord,
    And sometimes cheer the devil.

Whippoorwill.

Day is sinking.   Night is rising.
    Breezes whisper, " Peace, be still."
Now the mild command out-braving,
    Comes the voice of whippoorwill.
Clamorous the songs he sings us,
    As if weary of the calm,
As if darkness filled him strangely
    With defiance and alarm.

.   .   .   .

Human nature's sun is sinking ;
    Some one whispers, " Peace, be still."
Now I hear the voice of conscience,
    Human nature's whippoorwill.

Lilac.

When I inhale the fragrance
  Of lilac blooms so sweet,
My thoughts go quickly backward,
  A schoolhouse old I greet.

And reverently I linger,
  The place to me is dear ;
E'en now sweet childish echoes
  Are sounding in my ear.

Again I see my playmates,
  I ne'er shall see them more ;
Again we pluck the lilacs
  That blossomed by the door.

How often I have formed them
  In chains ; again I seem
To be adorned with lilacs,
  The present is a dream.

Ah, fragrant, purple lilac,
  Your slender chains have power
To bind me to my childhood ;
  I treasure you, sweet flower.

Mary.

In a lone, secluded valley,
    Far from clamor of a town,
Covered o'er with vines and flowers,
    Stood a cottage old and brown.

This was Mary's home; 'twas humble;
    Yet the music of the brooks
Cheered her soul, and rest was perfect
    In the quiet woodland nooks.

Though sometimes she grew uneasy,
    Longing far away to roam,
Bravely she concealed her longing,
    For she loved her country home.

Plain was Mary, shy, and hardly
    Daring to a stranger speak ;
Humble was she, like a flower,
    For she knew that she was weak.

Yet she dared be kind and loving,
    Dared to lighten others' care ;
And the valley lost its sunshine
    When it lost her presence fair.

Helpful was she, ready ever
　　To do all within her power—
Read or pray, or, if 'twas needed,
　　Watch the lonely midnight hour.

For the living toiled she gladly,
　　Flowers she gathered for the dead,
And the feeble, sick, and dying
　　Showered blessings on her head.

.　　.　　.　　.　　.　　.　　.　　.

Hushed the valley, stillness reigneth,
　　E'en the breeze is sadly sighing;
Every head is bowed with sorrow,
　　For "our Mary" now is dying.

She is dead.　A shadow resteth
　　O'er the valley; all is still,
Save the wailing of the breezes
　　Or the sobbing of the rill.

.　　.　　.　　.　　.　　.　　.　　.

Years have passed, and fickle Nature
　　Has forgot her sorrow now;
Breeze and brook are singing gaily,
　　Not a shadow clouds her brow.

Other faces cheer the valley,
　　Others laugh and sing and jest;
Mary, in her grave forgotten,
　　Lies in quiet, peaceful rest.

Lies forgotten.   No one mentions
  Aught of life so pure and fair,
No one knows her lone grave, passing,
  That a saint lies buried there.

Just a humble slab is able
  Mary's resting-place to tell,
And her grave is guarded only
  By the flowers she loved so well.

Heaven.

Some picture heaven a city,
　With many streets of gold,
With pearly gates, with mansions
　Whose beauties ne'er were told;
Some picture it a forest,
　Where many flowers blow,
Where bright-winged birds are singing,
　With music soft and low.

Some picture heaven a resting-place,
　Where with some well loved friend
They hold a sweet communion
　While heart with heart doth blend.
Some picture it a joyful place,
　Where music e'er is heard,
Where white-robed angels sweetly sing
　Till every pulse is stirred.

I know not, dare not, picture
　What heaven is to be;
But this I know, it perfect is,
　Prepared for you and me;
And Christ is there, a radiant light,
　Our friend, companion, lover,
And we fore'er content will be
　Around that light to hover.

The Child.

I love a child, I'll tell you why—
No vile deceit is in its eye,
Its soul is mirrored clear within,
Untarnished, free from any sin.

Its heart is spotless, free from guile,
Sincerity is in its smile ;
No flattery is in its words,
Its lispings are like notes of birds.

Like angels pure and undefiled,
The children tarry here a while
Before to realms of sin they fly.
I love a child, I've told you why.

Strange.

I shuddered as I saw it,
 A monster far away.
It nearer came! I trembled.
 Still nearer! Fearful? Nay!

When by my side it glistened,
 An angel brilliant, fair,
'Twas beautiful; its awfulness
 Had gone, I know not where.

White Violets.

Blue-veined and pure,
  Magical flower,
Not with haughtiness
  Dost thou tower.

Humble art thou,
  Lowly and good.
Thy sweetness telleth
  Thy neighborhood.

Blue Violets.

I heard sweet voices singing,
  With music soft and sweet;
I saw the singers standing
  And trembling at my feet.

A silence, then I listened,
  But not a sound I heard,
Save the murmur of a brooklet
  Or the flutter of a bird.

"Sing on, sweet ones," I whispered,
  "My heart is filled with love
For you, dear little blessings,
  Emblems of heaven above.

"Fear not!   I will not pluck you;
  Know that I am your friend.
Sing on, let your sweet voices
  In fearless music blend."

I listened in amazement
  As through those woody dells
There rose the sweetest music,
  Like ringing silver bells.

Do you not know the singers—
  The flowers of azure hue,
The blooms which sing of springtime,
  The violets of blue?

Cynicism.

Life is vapid, life is wretched!
   Death alone us honor brings.
Yet we shrink from death, but to life
   How the meanest mortal clings.

Land of Imagination.

A dazzling, fantastical land,
Ideal and supermundane ;
Cymophanous and brilliant,
Inhabited by the insane.

Trust.

Question not your Maker's business,
  Know you not that he is just?
He has made you, he can keep you;
  Place your hand in his and trust.

Money.

Money is a bird,
  Teach it how to fly,
Send it out into the world,
  Send it up on high ;
Then it will come flying back,
  All your virtues singing,
And, I doubt not, many pearls
  For your crown be bringing.

Do not cage the bird,
  Surely as you do,
It will toss itself about
  Till it forces through.
Then it never will return,
  Though for it you die ;
Do not cage your bird of wealth,
  Teach it how to fly.

Presentiment.

Presentiment is that dark cloud,
   That swiftly is appearing;
Which, threatening, silent, tells the soul
   A gathering storm is nearing.

Don't Be Deceived.

Youth has many dreams of love,
Like clouds across the sky above,
   Beautiful but fleeting.
But some day youth from dreams will wake,
When true love comes the heart to take,
   The very life completing.

Dandelion.

I saw a sturdy dandelion,
  With hair than gold more bright.
A week passed on, his golden hair
  Was turned to silken white.

Another week, his poll was bare;
  Another—where was he ?
Ah, dandelion, strangely you
  Prefigure life to me.

Day and Night.

A dazzling queen, with rosy face,
  With hair of gold and garments light,
Approached the earth with fairy tread,
  And thus addressed her sister, Night:

"Away, vile sister, get you hence!
  You bring but woe and crime and shame,
You shield the drunkard and the thief,
  You blast and darken many a name.

" Give place to me. I come with cheer,
  I come with hope and truth and light,
Your hidden crimes I will reveal—
  Away with you, foul, cruel Night."

The cheek of Night grew pale with grief,
  Her teardrops fell on flower and grass,
She spoke: "O fair-faced sister Day,
  Hear but a word before I pass.

" I am not all accursed, for souls
  Who, weary, long for sleep and rest,
With gladness see thee pass, and hail
  My coming, call me sweet and blest.

"I shield the wrong, I cover crime;
  But crimes which only God can see,
The vilest crimes by earth o'erlooked,
  Fair sister, refuge find with thee."

Day answered not. Night disappeared.
  The world awoke; all life was stirred.
Those ardent words of Day and Night
  No ear save mine and Nature's heard.

"In Union Is Strength."

" 'Tis time," proclaimed a snowflake,
  As through the cloud he whirled,
" For us to join together
  And subdue the dying world.

" Let us unite together,
  And fall with all our might,
And e'er another morning
  We will hide the earth from sight."

So the snowflakes rushed together,
  And fell with all their might—
With Frost for king, fell bravely down,
  And covered earth from sight.

A Special Place.

Come now, cast off your gloom,
  With smiles now wreathe your face ;
Throw off this spirit of unrest,
  You're needed in your place.
Has Christ not said, " I will prepare
  A place for you in heaven "?
Then surely on this earth to you
  A special place is given.

Anywhere.

Anywhere 'neath heaven's blue
There is something good to do.

Showers of Blessing.

You say there are dark clouds around you,
　　That God does not hear when you call?
Be still; were there ne'er clouds above you,
　　No showers of blessing would fall!

To a Pansy.

(On a sunny day.)

Dear little flower, how lovely you are.
Your tiny bright face makes me think of a star.

Your manner is winning, your heart is light,
And the smile on your face is happy and bright.

Sweet little pansy, your beauty I love,
I regard you a gift from our Father above.

To a Pansy.

(On a rainy day.)

High-colored flower, ungraceful of shape,
Your impudent face makes me think of an ape.

My heart is lonely and sad as can be,
And here you stand, making faces at me.

Pansy, I hate you; I'm sure I don't know
Why God ever suffered such a rude flower to
    blow.

Unheard Melodies.

Our hearts are enriched by the music
   That comes from the throat of a bird.
O what of the infinite sweetness
   Of melodies by us unheard !

A Lesson.

I saw a gipsy woman,
  . A wretched creature, wild,
With shabby dress, and holding
  By one gaunt hand, a child.

A stately lady neared her ;
  One glance of scorn she cast,
Then drew her skirts around her,
  And proudly glided past.

Just then a ray of sunlight
  Streamed at the gipsy's feet,
And brightened all her path. The child
  Sprang forward, merry, fleet,

And tried to grasp its brightness.
  The mother sadly smiled—
And then the sunbeam passed to shade,
  And it was not defiled.

Stamped.

There was a coin stamped and bright,
　'Twas crushed beneath the ground,
'Twas weather-rusted, still a coin ;
　The stamp can there be found.

There is a soul, all sin-begrimed,
　That never breathed a prayer.
Be patient, for it is a soul ;
　God's stamp is surely there.

Nature Breaks Her Fast.

Lift the cover off her dish,
   Nature's night is past.
Now she, rising, waiting, stands,
   See her break her fast.

First with fingers wet with dew
   She throws away the night,
Then with brightly beaming face,
   Clad in garments light,

Eats her breakfast, fog and clouds,
   Mixed with shade and sun ;
Then she drinks, from flowery cups,
   Dewdrops, every one.

An Object Lesson.

A goblet filled with crystal clear,
   With water pure as truth,
But represents with vivid force
   The purity of youth—
Youth, ere the stain and force of sin
   Has entered in the soul ;
Youth filled with purity and life,
   Complete in Christ, and whole.

Another goblet here appears,
   With liquid red within.
This represents with no less force
   The awfulness of sin ;
And just one drop of liquid red,
   If dropped in liquid clear,
Will change the color of the whole,
   And stained 'twill all appear.

'Tis colored now, no longer pure.
   The drop of red so small
Has stealthily crawled through the whole,
   And changed the water all.
Now what will take it out again,
   And make it all appear
Again the symbol of fair youth,
   Like water, pure and clear ?

Water can do it, see it now,
  As the water floweth in,
The red is swiftly running out,
  Now all is clear within.
Ah, see ! 'tis full, 'tis running o'er,
  'Tis flowing in the bowl.
And so it is with human life—
  With man's immortal soul.

Aye, so it is with human life—
  One sinful deed, 'tis true,
Will mar the beauty of the soul,
  And permeate it through.
Then, youth, beware ; O trifle not
  With sin, however slight,
For it will mar your purity
  And drive away the right.

But Christ has said, " Whoever will
  May come to me and live,
May freely drink the stream of life ;
  His sins I will forgive.
And, though your sins like scarlet be,
  Come unto me, and know
That I can make them white as wool,
  Can make them like the snow."

Then, sinner, come ; His promise claim,
  With every sin now part.
Bid Christ come in, to dwell within
  And purify your heart.
Drink freely from the stream of life,
  And do not be sufficed
Till you are full and running o'er
  With life and love of Christ.

Hate.

Hate is that rumbling monster
Who hurled the flashing dagger
  That pierced the heavens,
  And drenched the earth,
And made you homeward stagger.

Missionary Lesson from Nature.

Nature holds the sweetest lessons
   For the aged and the young,
If we but with love translate her,
   We shall hear a heavenly tongue.
Underneath a stone some flowers,
   Dying, crushed in bondage, lay ;
With but thoughts of love and pity,
   Quick I rolled the stone away.

With the sunlight's beams upon them,
   Soon they flourished, soon they grew ;
This the lesson Nature gave me,
   Which in turn I give to you :
Like those flowers souls are dying,
   Crushed by darkness worse than night ;
Hasten, free them from their bondage,
   Tell them of our God, our light !

Thanksgiving.

Ye who dwell in homes of comfort,
   Having every want supplied,
Who with parents, brothers, sisters,
   Are contented, satisfied,
Pause a moment in your gladness,
   Lift your hearts to God above,
All these countless blessings reach you
   From the fullness of his love.

Ye who dwell in humble dwellings,
   Shiv'ring, cold, and hungry too,
Still be thankful, and remember
   That your Father cares for you.
Thank him, for above in splendor
   Is a mansion firm and sure,
Which for you is waiting, waiting,
   And which will fore'er endure.

Story of Life

Morning, springtime, flowers budding,
    Sparkling grass, dew diamonds bright,
Here, a river sparkles gaily,
    There, a cottage is in sight;
From the cottage steps a vision,
    Vision of sweet childhood's grace,
Floating hair and brown eyes fearless,
    And a merry, laughing face.

Footstep light and form of willow,
    To a mead she wends her way;
Gathers pebbles, buds, and grasses,
    And then, weary of her play,
Lies beneath a bush of rosebuds,
    Soon is resting, fast asleep,
Happily in dreamland wanders,
    While the angels vigil keep.
          .   .   .   .

Noonday, summer, flowers blooming,
    By a fragrant rosebush fair
Stands a lover, youthful, manly,
    And a girl with golden hair.
He is speaking, bending, earnest.
    "Yes," she whispers, soft and sweet.
Hand in hand they leave the roses,
    Paths unknown to them they greet.

.   .   .   .

Autumn.   Ah, the day is fading,
    Yet the ripened fruit doth wave,
And beneath the leafless rosebush
    Is a lonely, silent grave.
O'er it kneels a black-robed woman—
    Kneeling, sobs her life away,
While the golden sun is setting
    And while shadows fill the day.

.   .   .   .

Winter, evening, snow is falling,
    All the landscape gleams with white,
And the earth is cold and deathlike,
    Not a rosebush is in sight.
Childhood, youth, and age have vanished
    Yet a picture meets our gaze—
Like a gate to joys immortal,
    Side by side two silent graves.

Rest and Work.

What is rest ?   'Tis change of labor,
   Hoping, loving, day by day.
What is work ?   'Tis constant worship,
   Prayer unceasing—let us pray.

Atlantic.

I've fallen in love with a rough old chap,
   He is black and blue and green,
And boisterous, and so very large
   That his half was never seen.

He roars at me both day and night,
   I love him just the same.
You will not wonder when I say,
   Atlantic is his name.

Cloud-Edens.

[Class Poem, New Hampton, June 23, 1892.]

Morning dawned.   The brilliant sunbeams
　　Flooded all the land with light ;
Blue and clear the sky above, and
　　Not a cloud was there in sight.
Peaceful, tranquil, like an Eden
　　Was the morning, calm and clear ;
Yet unseen the clouds were gathering,
　　And a storm was brooding near.

Ere the sun had reached the zenith
　　Gloomy shadows like a shroud
Veiled the world, its sunny Eden
　　Was but resting on a cloud.
Soon the sky above was darkened,
　　Clouds its azure hid from view ;
Fiercely then the storm descended,
　　Frightened birds then homeward flew.

Soon the world was filled with beauty,
　　Clearer, grander, than before,
And a gleaming bow of promise
　　Told the soul the storm was o'er ;
While the brightened world seemed saying,
　　" Storms are blessings in disguise ;
Men and birds and flowers would perish
　　Were there always sunny skies."

Classmates in this verdant valley,
   Which like Eden seems to me,
We have lived as in the sunlight,
   Scarce a shadow could we see;
Yet unseen the clouds were gath'ring,
   Brooding, darkening, and to-day
Full the storm has burst upon us—
   Is there in our sky one ray

Of bright sunlight yet to cheer us?
   'Neath the clouds so dark and drear,
Is a gleaming rainbow hiding?
   Is there gladness to appear?
Ah, to-day the sky is darkened,
   Yet within its misty haze
Pictures dimly from the future
   Seem to meet my ardent gaze.

In the distance, faces smiling,
   Half-unseen, appear to me;
Gleaming, bright air-castles, classmates,
   On Ambition's hill I see.
Onward, then, ascend the mountain,
   Do not fear the tempests loud;
But, when you have reached your Eden.
   Know 'tis resting on a cloud.

Though we leave this little village,
  Oft we'll linger here again ;
Of this dear old Institution
  Tender memories will remain.
To this quiet, peaceful valley
  Fondly e'er our hearts will cling.
Oft we'll hear the church bell tolling,
  Oft we'll hear our school bell ring.

We must part, and though the future
  Bring us glory, wealth, and fame—
Or, if we should fall from honor,
  Earn and bear a tarnished name—
Yet sweet memories will bind us
  With the chains of love and truth,
We can ne'er forget our classmates
  And the school-days of our youth.

E'en when age with snowy fingers
  Shall have touched our hair with white,
Memories still will cheer our pathway,
  As the moon illumes the night.
And as to the misty future
  Dimly now our fancies tend,
May we take with us our motto,
  " Let us on ourselves depend."

And though every golden sunbeam
   Must be hidden by a shroud,
And though every earthly Eden
   Is o'ershadowed by a cloud,
Yet sweet Nature oft has taught us
   That no storm can long abide,
That beneath the clouds which bind us
   Lovingly the sunbeams hide.

Introspection.

I read the thoughts of great poets,
   For me there's a pearl in each line ;
I read them, I learn them, repeat them,
   Till it seems as if their thoughts are mine.
And then fond hopes come stealing upon me,
   And a voice whispers low in my ear,
" You too shall sing sweet songs of magic,
   And your songs the whole world shall hear."

Who is it that whispered ?   'Tis Fancy.
   And I clasp her close to my breast ;
She fills me with happiness, misery,
   With hopefulness, tumult, unrest ;
And I question, "And will it be, Fancy,
   That I such sweet meters will sing
That all the world humbly will listen ?
   Will they riches and fame to me bring ?

Then sadly sweet Fancy made answer,
   "Look into your heart ; is it pure ?
Are you trying to win earthly honor,
   Or riches which e'er will endure ?
Are you looking to Jesus to help you,
   Is your heart with God's beauty aflame,
Or is it earth's treasures you're seeking—
   Earth's riches, earth's honor, earth's fame ? "

Her voice was like magic. I listened,
   Then answered, "Ah, Fancy, you know
How God's mercy, his goodness and justice,
   Just makes my full heart overflow.
In each flower, in each leaf is a poem,
   I long its true meaning to find ;
I long to translate Nature truly,
   I long to give sight to the blind.

" I long to sing balm for the weary,
   I long to give hope to the sad,
I long to give faith to the doubting,
   I long to bring grace for the bad,
I long to sing songs which will strengthen,
   Which will guide souls to heaven above,
I long to make everyone purer,
   For my heart is o'erflowing with love."

God help me to sing songs of magic,
   But make all my singing a loss,
If I glory in aught save Christ Jesus,
   His life, his perfection, his cross.
Inspire me, O God, with thy spirit,
   While I rest and learn at thy feet.
Let thy heart and my heart and Nature's
   Beat together in unison sweet.

www.ingramcontent.com/pod-product-compliance
Lightning Source LLC
Chambersburg PA
CBHW021111020726
47500CB00003B/699